The
Great Howling
Mystery

Jo Cotterill

Illustrated by
Oscar Price

OXFORD
UNIVERSITY PRESS

Great Clarendon Street, Oxford, OX2 6DP,
United Kingdom

Oxford University Press is a department of the University of Oxford.
It furthers the University's objective of excellence in research, scholarship,
and education by publishing worldwide. Oxford is a registered trade mark of
Oxford University Press in the UK and in certain other countries

Text © Jo Cotterill 2017

Illustrations © Oscar Price 2017

The moral rights of the author have been asserted

First published 2017

British Library Cataloguing in Publication Data
Data available

978-0-19-837764-1

1 3 5 7 9 10 8 6 4 2

Paper used in the production of this book is a natural, recyclable product
made from wood grown in sustainable forests. The manufacturing process
conforms to the environmental regulations of the country of origin.

Printed in China by Leo Paper Products Ltd.

Acknowledgements
Inside cover notes written by Karra McFarlane

Contents

Chapter 1
So Many Dogs

Dogs. Big dogs, small dogs, long-haired dogs, yappy dogs. Tyla gave a sigh as she watched them go by. It was such bad luck that her brother Ash was allergic to dogs.

She sat on the park bench and swung her legs. Beside her, Ash was playing a game on his tablet. She could imagine the sounds it was making: *Bang! Squish! Dah, dah, daaaah!* But she couldn't hear any of it. Instead, she watched the people walking their dogs.

Tyla knew all
the dogs in this area.
There was Benson,
the collie, who
loved to jump into
the lake and get
very wet and muddy.

There was Tess,
the black poodle,
who looked like she
walked on tiptoes
all the time.

There was
Wallace, the Great
Dane, who was so
strong she could pull
her owner right over.

Tyla smiled. One of her very favourite dogs had just turned up: Bug the pug. Bug was called Bug because of his enormous bug-like eyes.

Tyla waved at Bug's owner, Jacky, and patted Ash's arm.

He looked up. "What?"

Tyla pointed. "My favourite," she signed.

Ash saw Bug and grinned. "He would be a rubbish pet," he signed back to his sister. "He's so smelly."

"I wouldn't care!" Tyla's hands were a blur as she made the words. "He's just the right size to cuddle."

Ash rolled his eyes. "There's no point thinking about it," he told her. "I'm still allergic."

Tyla sighed. If she had a dog, she could teach it to do tricks. To jump through hoops, go through tunnels, walk on its hind legs. Plus, of course, it could help her cross the road, and wake her up if there was a fire – all useful things if you couldn't hear.

Sometimes Tyla liked to go to the animal rescue place in town. They had all kinds of dogs and cats and rabbits there, looking for a new home. It was a noisy place but that didn't bother Tyla. She always felt very sad when it was time to leave, because she knew none of those dogs would ever be hers.

Jacky and Bug came over. Bug wagged his stubby tail as Tyla patted him. Jacky said something but Tyla didn't understand. "Again?" she signed.

"I said," said Jacky, making her lips move slowly, "that he's getting fat. The vet says we have to walk him three times a day from now on."

Tyla laughed. "He'll like that," she signed, and Ash told Jacky what she'd said.

Jacky grinned back. "Yes, but I won't!"

Bug licked Tyla's face. She felt sad when Jacky took him off down the path.

Ash gave her a nudge. He was holding out his tablet. On the screen was a picture of a dog. Not an ordinary dog, but a robot dog.

Tyla glanced up at her brother.

"I'm not allergic to robots," he signed, raising his eyebrows. "And it says it can learn things."

Tyla's eyes opened wide, and she looked at the screen again. A robot dog that could learn tricks? That could be the answer to everything! She tapped the screen to see the price, and her heart sank.

Three hundred pounds! Where would they get that kind of money?

Chapter 2
A Disappearing Bug

"No," said Tyla's mum when they got home. "Not in a million years. Unless we win the lottery."

"You don't play the lottery," Tyla pointed out.

Her mum gave a sad kind of smile. "Sorry, love. Three hundred pounds is an awful lot."

"I'll help you save up," Ash said to Tyla. "I think having a robot dog would be cool!"

"How much money do you have?" Tyla asked.

They turned out Ash's money tin. "Three pounds twenty pence. It would have been more but I bought five strawberry laces yesterday."

"It's more than I have!" Tyla signed. "We'll just have to start saving up. Maybe we could get jobs."

"I know!" Ash suddenly looked excited. "You could offer to walk dogs for people! Jacky said she didn't want to walk Bug three times a day. *You* could do it!"

Tyla felt very happy. "Brilliant idea! Let's go over this evening and ask Jacky."

But when they got to Jacky's house, they found her in tears. "I've just come back from the police station," she said. "Bug's run off!"

"Oh no!" exclaimed Ash.

"Run off?" signed Tyla. "Are you sure? How did it happen?"

Jacky wiped her eyes. "It was the strangest thing," she said. "You'd better come in."

When they were sitting down, Jacky told them what had happened. "After I saw you at the park," Jacky began, "Bug and I went into the field at the end. You know, the one beside the woods.

I let him off the lead so he could have a run around. And then I heard this weird noise."

"What kind of noise?" asked Ash.

Jacky shook her head, frowning. "It was like … a howling. A loud, high howling. Like an animal in pain. It freaked me out. I thought it was a fox caught in a trap, something like that."

"What did you do?" Tyla signed. Ash translated for Jacky.

"I went to find it," Jacky said. "I looked and looked, but I couldn't find out where the howling noise was coming from. First it was in the hedge. Then it sounded like it was coming from further away. And then it just stopped. I never found an animal. And when I called to Bug …" Tears came to her eyes. "When I called to Bug, there was no reply. I don't know if he was frightened by the howling. I walked around for an hour, calling. But he never came." She burst into tears again. "He's gone!"

Chapter 3
The Search Begins

"Where could Bug have gone?" Tyla wondered. She and Ash were in their pyjamas. They were supposed to be going to sleep, but they were sitting up in their beds, signing to each other.

"He must have been scared off by the howling," Ash said. "Maybe he ran into the woods."

"Then why didn't he come back when the howling stopped and Jacky called him?" asked Tyla.

Ash shrugged. "Maybe he fell down a hole or got stuck in a bramble."

"Oh, poor Bug!" Tyla felt awful. "We should go and look for him tomorrow."

Ash jerked his head to the door and suddenly dived under his duvet. Tyla recognized the signal – Mum was coming! She just had time to lie down before the bedroom door opened.

Mum flicked on the main light. Tyla sneaked open one eye.

Mum was looking right at her. "I can hear your hands moving, you know," she signed, speaking at the same time. "Go to sleep!"

Tyla grinned into her pillow. She knew Mum was fibbing – no one could

hear hands moving through the air –
but Mum had an amazing ability to
know when they were staying up late.
Tyla yawned. Tomorrow they'd go out
and hunt for Bug. If they found him,
Jacky might be so grateful, she would let
Tyla take him for walks, and maybe pay
her too …

The next morning, Tyla and Ash went
over to visit Jacky. "He didn't come
home last night," said Jacky. She looked
pale and tired. "I don't know what to
do. Should I go out and look for him,
or should I stay here in case he finds his
own way home?"

"We'll go and look for him," Tyla told
her, with Ash translating. "Don't worry."

Jacky smiled in relief. "That's so kind
of you. Here …" She went and fetched a
handful of papers. "Can you stick these
up around the place too?"

It was a printout of a photo of Bug,
with some writing underneath:

Lost Dog

Bug the pug
Missing from Allen's
Field, Friday 4pm
Reward if found: £100

There was a telephone number too, but Tyla didn't notice it. "One hundred pounds!" she signed to Ash. "We could do with a hundred pounds!"

"For the robot dog! Yes!" Ash signed back.

Jacky hadn't understood the signing. "Do you have an idea about where he might be?" she asked hopefully.

Tyla felt bad. This wasn't about the money. It was about a lost friend. "We will do our best," she told Jacky, and Ash translated.

"Thank you," Jacky said, and they left before she burst into tears again.

"Let's go along the High Street," Ash said, as they set off. "We should put these posters up first. Then we'll go to the woods."

"OK." Tyla nodded.

Everyone they met was very kind and sympathetic. Before long, fifteen posters were up around the town, and lots of

people promised to keep an eye out
for Bug.

Tyla and Ash went out to the field where Bug had gone missing. There was no sign of him, or of any hurt animal that might have been howling. They went into the woods but after an hour of searching and calling, they gave up.

"I feel terrible," Tyla signed as they headed home, their feet hurting. "Poor Jacky."

"At least everyone in the town knows to look out for Bug," Ash replied. "It's not like this place has much else to talk about!"

But he was wrong about that.

As they turned the corner into the High Street, they could see a big group of people standing outside the bookshop. Tyla and Ash pushed their way through. In the middle was Mr Webb with his two children, Clara and Jess. Clara and Jess were in tears, clutching a dog lead – with no dog on the end.

23

Tyla didn't know which way to look. Everyone was talking at once. "What's going on?" she signed to Ash.

"Another dog has gone missing!" he signed back quickly. "The Webbs' Dalmatian, Soozy. Over by the business park this time. Mr Webb says ... hang on." Ash broke off to listen.

Tyla waited impatiently. Mr Webb had a thick moustache, so she couldn't read his lips. What was he saying?

When Ash turned back to her, he looked stunned. "You'll never believe it," he signed to her. "But the same thing happened! Mr Webb says they heard a strange howling noise, right before Soozy disappeared!"

Tyla's mouth fell open. The same howling noise? And a disappearing dog? It couldn't be coincidence! What on earth was going on?

Chapter 4
Going, Going ... Gone!

Over the next three days, three more dogs disappeared. First it was Petra, a tiny chihuahua. Next, Toby the Jack Russell. Then Tess, the black poodle. Every single one of them had disappeared after hearing the strange howling noise.

Now there were groups of people out looking for the dogs every day, and posters on every lamp post and in every shop window. No one dared to let their dog off the lead any more.

"The reward money is going up," reported Ash. "If we found all the dogs, we'd easily have enough to buy our robot dog."

"Don't," Tyla signed, upset. "It's all so awful. Those poor frightened dogs. Where can they be?"

"Someone must know," said Ash.

"Come on. Mum asked us to take this pie over to Jacky's."

Jacky looked like she hadn't slept since Bug disappeared. "Your mother is very kind," she said, taking the pie and putting it in the washing machine.

Tyla took the pie out of the machine and put it in the fridge. "Still no word, then?" she signed with Ash translating.

Jacky shook her head, but before she could say anything, something caught her attention and she headed to the front door. Then something amazing happened. Jacky opened the door, and there on the top step was Bug the pug! Jacky fell to her knees, hugging Bug who licked her face and wagged his stumpy little tail so hard it almost fell off.

Tyla couldn't make out anything Jacky was saying, but standing behind Bug was a young woman. She was about medium height, with short red hair and purple glasses. She was wearing a green jacket and blue jeans and she was smiling. "I'm guessing this is the right house, then," she said, and Tyla was pleased that she could read her lips very easily.

Jacky stood up, and before the young woman could say anything else, Jacky hugged her too!

Tyla didn't see what Jacky said, but the woman replied, "Oh, I found him wandering along the road to Whitsby. I took him to the vet. Everyone there said I should bring him along to you." She smiled at Tyla. "So here I am!"

Tyla smiled back. The young woman was very pretty. She had a funny way of twisting her mouth on the letter 'r', but Tyla could still see what she said.

Jacky didn't want to let go of Bug even for a second, so she sent Ash to fetch the money from her kitchen – one hundred pounds

in ten pound notes. The woman smiled even more as she took it. "I'm studying at university," she said. "This will really help!"

As Tyla and Ash walked home, Tyla felt more hopeful about the missing dogs. "Someone is looking after them," she signed to her brother. "Did you see how well Bug looked? Someone's been feeding him. Tomorrow, we should go to the road where he was found. Maybe there'll be a clue."

"We could still win some reward money," said Ash. "Four dogs are still missing!"

But the next day, two of them came back.

Chapter 5
Howling Behind
a Gate

Tyla and Ash were on their way back from the park when they saw a young man walk up the path to Mrs Teesdale's house. Trotting along beside him was Tess, the missing black poodle! Tyla grabbed Ash's arm, and together they hurried over. The front door opened, and Mrs Teesdale let out a scream before falling to her knees to hug her excited dog.

"Oh, thank you," sobbed Mrs Teesdale. "Oh, Tess! I've been so worried!" She looked up at the man. "She's my best friend, you know. Been with me for nine years, ever since my husband died."

Tyla and Ash stared at the young man who had brought back the missing dog. He had untidy brown hair and a little moustache, like he was trying to look more grown-up than he actually was.

"Where did you find her?" Ash asked.

"Out near the business park," Tyla saw the man's lips say. "Just ambling along, you know. Like he didn't realize he was lost."

"It's a girl dog," Tyla signed, but the man didn't understand.

Mrs Teesdale held out some notes. "This is yours."

"Oh," said the man, "I don't need paying, that's all right."

"Take it," she insisted. "It's the least I can do."

"Well, if you say so," he said, pocketing the money. "Just glad to have been of service. See you!" He gave a cheery wave and went on his way. Mrs Teesdale ushered Tess inside the house, shutting the door firmly behind her.

Ash frowned. "This is all very weird. Bug was found on the road to Whitsby. Tess was found on the other side of town. And I heard that Petra turned up this morning too, hiding in someone's empty dustbin on South Street. How did they get there?"

"All that lovely reward money," said Tyla with a sigh. "And none of it for us! If only we'd been in those places at the right time!"

They walked back along the High Street. Ellen Castle was peering into the window of the shoe shop. Her German shepherd dog, Frank, sat patiently at her feet. She gave a wistful sigh as Tyla and Ash reached her.

"So pretty," she murmured.

Then she turned and saw them. "Tyla, Ash, help me! I want to buy shoes I don't need. Will you walk with me up the hill to distract me?"

Tyla and Ash grinned. Ellen Castle already had a lot of shoes!

The three of them started up the hill, Frank loping alongside. As they drew level with a house with a red front door, Ellen and Ash stopped so suddenly that Tyla bumped into them. She pulled at Ash's sleeve and made a 'what's up?' face.

"I can hear something," he signed to her, his head on one side. "Like … someone in pain. Whimpering. It's coming from behind the garden gate. Someone needs help!"

Ellen thrust Frank's lead into Tyla's hand. "Hold him," she said so that Tyla could read her lips. Tyla nodded and looked down at Frank, who didn't seem in the least bothered by the noise that the others could hear.

A young woman in running gear was jogging along the pavement, a blonde ponytail bobbing out behind her. She slowed down as she reached Tyla, and smiled at her. "Hello!" she said cheerfully. "Is this your dog?"

Tyla shook her head and pointed at Ellen.

The jogger bent down to stroke Frank. Then she looked up and said, "I wish I could have a dog. Everyone should have a pet."

There was something about the woman that puzzled Tyla, but just then, Ash tugged on her arm. "Come and help," he signed.

Tyla bent down and tied Frank's lead

to the fence. The jogger stood up. Tyla smiled at her and went to help the others.

Ellen was trying to force the side gate open with a chunky stick. Ash signed to Tyla, "I think we can get over the gate if we drag the wheelie bin to it. Then I can climb on top …"

Tyla nodded to show she understood, and together they dragged the heavy wheelie bin over to the gate. Ash started to climb up. Tyla glanced back at the road – and froze.

Frank's lead hung from the fence – but Frank was no longer attached to it.

Chapter 6
A Breakthrough

Tyla rushed back to the road, looking frantically from left to right. There, in the distance, was Frank. He was lolloping along after the jogger, but the next second they were both out of sight.

"Ash!" yelled Tyla, setting off after Frank. Her feet thudded along the pavement, and her breaths came in great gasps, but when she reached the end of the street, there was no sign of either the jogger or the dog.

Ash panted up behind her. "What happened?"

"I lost him!" Tyla signed, almost in tears. "That woman – she took him!"

Ash looked shocked. "Took him? What do you mean? Why?"

But Tyla was standing completely still, eyes wide, staring at nothing. She'd just realized what had puzzled her about the woman. "The letter 'r'!" she mouthed to herself.

Ash was baffled. "The what?"

Tyla grabbed Ash's arm so tightly that he winced. Her brain was going at the speed of a rocket. The jogger … her mouth had twisted on the word 'everyone'. Just like the woman who'd returned Bug to Jacky. Both of them had the same strange way of forming the letter 'r'. But … they were two completely different people.

Weren't they?

Ash waved a hand in front of his sister's face. "Hello in there? What's going on?"

Tyla let go of his arm, to his relief. Rapidly, she started to sign. "The jogger – she took Frank! I think she's the same person who brought Bug back. The dogs aren't running away. They're being stolen! That woman is stealing the dogs; then she disguises herself and returns them! She's doing it all for the reward money!"

Ash looked incredulous. "But it can't all be the same person! That jogger had blonde hair. The woman who brought back Bug had red hair. And the man who found Tess – well, he was a man!"

Tyla's brain gave another jolt. In her memory, she could see the young man, taking Mrs Teesdale's money … his little scrubby moustache that looked almost pretend … she'd spent so much time looking at the moustache, she hadn't really noticed the way he used his lips … but yes! He had done the same thing with the letter 'r'!

"He's the same person too!" insisted Tyla. "It was the woman dressed up, I just know it! We have to tell the police!"

Chapter 7
Telling the Police

Sergeant Patel wasn't very impressed. He was a big man with very thick eyebrows, which frowned a lot at Tyla as she explained.

"The same person?" he said, disbelieving. "That's impossible. The three people who returned the dogs were all different."

"She's really good at disguise," Tyla signed for Ash to translate. "You can change your hair and your clothes and put make-up on and all that – but you can't change the way your mouth makes letters. Everyone does it differently."

Sergeant Patel shook his head. "I'm sure you're an expert, Tyla, but this is ridiculous. You can't go around accusing people without proof. The dogs hear a noise that upsets them, and they run away."

"That's not how it happens!" protested Tyla.

Sergeant Patel placed his hands on the desk. "Thank you for coming in," he said, "but I think you've got too much imagination."

Tyla was fuming as they left the police station. "Too much imagination?"

"Calm down," Ash signed back. "There's nothing we can do."

Tyla shook her head angrily. "There must be something. Who's going to stop this woman stealing more dogs and collecting the rewards?"

"It must be costing her a fortune in dog food," Ash commented.

Tyla gasped. "Of course! She's having to feed them and look after them. Ash, this is our chance."

"Our chance to what?"

Tyla beamed at her brother. "To catch the thief!"

Chapter 8
Following a Clue

Ash followed along behind Tyla, but since she wasn't looking at him, she could ignore his protests entirely.

Now, which shop should she start with? There were three that sold dog food: a small supermarket on the High Street, an animal supplies shop down a side street, and a big superstore on the outskirts of town.

The small supermarket was closest. Tyla set off. Ash grabbed her arm and forced her to stop. "You can't go off like this," he signed to her. "We're due home. Mum will be cross if we're late."

"It won't take long," Tyla told him. "You go home, so Mum doesn't worry. I'll be back in half an hour."

Ash frowned. "Tyla, don't you think you're taking this too far?"

Tyla glowered. "You don't believe me."

"I just think—"

But Tyla turned her back on him and stomped away. Now even her own brother didn't trust her!

Tyla always kept a pad of paper and a pencil in her pocket, so that she could write messages for people who didn't understand her signing. Now she got them out to write a note.

Hello. My name is Tyla and I'm doing a survey for school. It's about pet food. Can you tell me the most popular brand of dog food and how many tins you sell every day? Also, whether you have sold more tins recently.

The sales assistant at the supermarket smiled at her. "Of course," she said. "Let me fetch my manager."

The manager wrote down her answer:

Our most popular brand is Rover and we sell about ten tins every day. Our sales have been normal recently.

Tyla thanked them and left the shop, frowning. Not that shop, then. She continued on to the animal supplies shop. Of course, if that wasn't the right place either, then she'd have to ask Mum to take her to the superstore on the outskirts of town. That would be annoying.

But at the animal shop she had
good luck.

The kind lady with frizzy hair wrote:

Our most popular brand is
King. We sometimes sell lots
and we sometimes don't sell any.
You can get it cheaper at the
supermarket! But in the last
week we have sold lots and lots,
which makes my bank manager
very happy.

Tyla felt her spirits lift. They'd sold lots more than usual recently! Maybe to someone who was keeping a lot of dogs …?

She nearly bumped into someone in a brown coat as she was leaving the shop. "Oh, sorry," she saw the other person say.

Tyla felt as though something cold had just been tipped down her back. A word with the 'r' sound in it … and the customer's lips had twisted on it …

Heart racing, she went outside the shop and took great gulps of air. The dognapper was right here, right now, in the shop! She peeked through the window. He was buying dog food! Tyla jerked back as he turned around. If it hadn't been for the mouth, she'd never have recognized him – or her. Tyla reminded herself that it was a woman dressed up as a man. The disguise was so convincing!

The window frame vibrated as the
shop door closed, and the man started
off down the road.

What should she do? If she went
home to fetch Ash, she'd lose the thief!

There was nothing for it. Tyla set off
after the man in the brown coat.

Chapter 9
A Discovery

Tyla had never followed anyone before –
not in the *following a criminal* kind of
way – and it was far more difficult than
she expected.

The man in the brown coat walked
down the High Street. He turned left
and then right. Tyla felt puzzled. They
were still on streets with lots of houses.
How could anyone hide dogs here
without anyone else knowing?

The next moment, she had her
answer! The man stopped right
outside the house next to the animal
rescue place. Tyla almost groaned
with understanding. If you wanted
somewhere to hide barking dogs, then
the best place would be near other dogs,
wouldn't it?

The man went around the side of the
house and disappeared. Tyla wasn't sure

what to do. Did she have time to run
home and fetch help?

The man in the brown coat was
coming out again! He was no longer
carrying the bags of dog food.

Tyla quickly hid behind a parked car until the man was a long way down the street. Now was her chance! Tyla's heart thumped as she ran to the side of the house. She pushed open the wooden gate and gasped.

Three dogs were tied up in makeshift shelters in the garden – and they were barking and wagging their tails as hard as they could. She had found the missing dogs!

Chapter 10
Stop Thief!

Tyla couldn't keep the smile off her face as she walked up the High Street. Frank, Toby the Jack Russell and Soozy pulled hard on their leads, delighted to be out for a walk and eager to get home. Tyla could hardly believe that she'd just walked in and stolen the dogs back!

It took only minutes for the word to spread, and before long Ellen Castle, Toby's owner Mrs Okoro, and the Webb children came running up the street, arms wide to hug their pets. Sergeant Patel turned up too, looking a lot less frowny and a lot more friendly. Tyla tried to tell him where she'd found the dogs, but he couldn't understand her signing.

And then – Tyla saw the man in the brown coat! He was coming out of the little supermarket and when he saw the

crowd around the dogs, his mouth fell
open in shock. He turned abruptly and
started to walk away.

"Stop!" shouted Tyla. She grabbed
Sergeant Patel. "Him – there!" She
pointed urgently and pushed the
sergeant towards the man. "He's getting
away!" she signed.

But before the sergeant could react, Ash came tearing down the street on his bicycle. He shot past the astonished crowd and skidded to a halt, right in front of the man in the brown coat. "Don't go anywhere!" he cried.

As the man hesitated, Sergeant Patel ran over. "I'm sorry, sir, I'm going to have to ask you a few questions."

"Ash!" Tyla rushed over to her brother. "You came back!"

He grinned at her. "I felt bad for not believing you."

"This man is really a woman," Tyla signed to Sergeant Patel. Ash translated. "She's in disguise. Take off the hair!"

"What's going on?" cried the man angrily. But Ash reached over and tugged hard on the man's brown hair — and it came off in his hand! Underneath was short, blonde hair. And now it was obvious that she was a woman!

"You stole all the dogs," Tyla signed

crossly, with Ash translating. "And then you claimed the reward money. You are a horrible person!"

The woman glared at Tyla. "You can't prove anything!" She put her hand in her pocket nervously.

"Oh yeah? What have you got in your pocket?" Ash demanded.

Sergeant Patel frowned. "I think you'd better show us."

The woman gave a big sigh and pulled out her hand. In it was a small black machine. She pressed a button, and although Tyla couldn't hear the sound, she could guess what it was.

"The howling!" cried Sergeant Patel.

After the thief was taken away, Tyla and Ash walked home with a crowd of cheering dog owners. Tyla felt like she was walking on air. Together, she and Ash had solved a real mystery. There was only one thing that could ever top this as the best day …

***

A week later, there was a delivery for Tyla.

The box was big, and it just said, 'With grateful thanks from all your doggy friends' on it. What could it be?

A robot dog, of course! The perfect reward!

About the author

I love dogs. When I was young, my family had a dog called Tammy, who was very clever. Tammy could find her way home hours after disappearing into the woods at the bottom of the garden. I also love mystery books and would secretly like to be a detective. All the best detectives are really good at noticing things, which is why I decided to write about a deaf character because often people who are deaf are extra-talented noticers.

I have been writing books for over ten years and love it more than my previous jobs, which include acting and teaching. My latest book is about a girl who becomes a superhero and is called *Electrigirl*. I live in Oxfordshire with my family (but sadly no dogs).